L-I-T *Guide*
Literature In Teaching

Sounder
By William H. Armstrong

A Study Guide for Grades 4 and Up

Prepared by Charlotte S. Jaffe & Barbara T. Roberts

Illustrated by Karen Neulinger

ISBN 0-910857-86-5

© 1991 Educational Impressions, Inc., Hawthorne, NJ

EDUCATIONAL IMPRESSIONS, INC.
Hawthorne, NJ 07507

Sounder
Written by William H. Armstrong

STORY SUMMARY

William H. Armstrong tells us in the Author's Note that this is not his story, but rather one told to him as a boy by an old black teacher...

In this story, a poor black sharecropper family struggles to survive in the early part of the twentieth century. At times it is difficult to feed and clothe the family. Therefore, their coon dog Sounder becomes a provider of sorts. The animals he hunts are eaten, sold or traded for other necessities.

On one occasion, the father steals a ham in order to provide food for his family. He is later arrested for this theft. During the arrest, Sounder is shot. He disappears and when he finally returns home, he is badly injured.

When the father is taken from the jail to a prison work camp, the oldest son goes on many journeys searching for him. Although he is not successful in locating the camp, on his way home from one of these trips, he does meet a teacher who greatly affects his life. The boy always wanted to attend school on a regular basis, but circumstances had made it impossible. The teacher offers him a chance to have the education he always wanted.

Several years later, the father is injured at the prison work camp and returns home. A few months after his return, he dies. Shortly after the father's death, Sounder dies too.

Meet the Author
William H. Armstrong

William Armstrong began life as a farmboy in Lexington, Virginia, in 1914. He attended Bible classes at his local Presbyterian church, where he became familiar with the stories that he later retold in *Sounder*.

As a teen-ager, Armstrong attended a military school. His first attempt at story-writing was so good that his teachers refused to believe that he had written the story all by himself. Armstrong was greatly discouraged and he did not seriously write again until he was an adult.

After graduating from Hampden-Sydney College, Armstrong decided to become a teacher. He worked as a history master at the Kent School in Kent, Connecticut. Armstrong later continued his studies at the graduate school of the University of Virginia.

In 1942 Armstrong married Martha Williams and they had three children: Christopher, David and Mary. Two of them became artists and the other, a criminologist. Armstrong first wrote books and journal articles on varied educational subjects before trying his hand at a novel. He used his childhood memories of a neighbor's old coon dog with an unusual bark as an inspiration for his award-winning novel *Sounder*.

First published in 1969, *Sounder* was awarded the Newbery Medal and the Lewis Carroll Shelf Award. The children's editor of *The New York Times* Book Review called it the best novel of 1969. Other writings by the author include *Study Is Hard Work* (1956), *Through Troubled Waters* (1957), *Barefoot in the Grass—The Study of Grandma Moses* (1970) and *Tawny and Dingo* (1979).

Armstrong now enjoys tending his Corriedale sheep on a rocky slope in the Connecticut countryside. He resides in a stone home that he built himself.

Sharecropping

In the aftermath of the Civil War there developed in the rural part of the United States a system of farming known as sharecropping. Landowners rented out parcels of land to be farmed. In exchange for the use of the land and a cabin, the farmers, called sharecroppers, had to give the owner one half of the harvest. Usually, these sharecroppers raised cotton, tobacco or corn. They also kept a small vegetable garden for themselves. When there was a poor harvest, the farmers often had to go into debt to pay their shares. Most of the sharecroppers never managed to get out of debt to the landowners.

Sharecrop farming represented a harsh life. Families often lived in cramped quarters with only a few possessions and barely the necessities to sustain life. Most of their existence, time and energy were focused on the planting, cultivation and harvesting of crops and the provision of their own food and shelter. They had little time to devote to trying to change the political or social injustices of their lives.

Hunting dogs became very important to the sharecroppers and in many ways could be considered their prize possessions. The animals brought in by these dogs provided food for the family and also were traded for other necessities. Loss of a hunting dog would have been a great tragedy for its owner.

Vocabulary
Chapters One and Two

Draw a line from each vocabulary word on the left to its correct definition on the right.

1. quarry	A. where meat or fish is treated to keep from spoiling
2. persimmon	B. struggle to move without making progress
3. embrace	C. mournful; expressing sorrow
4. stern	D. confine; restrain
5. heritage	E. get back
6. precision	F. eager desire to know
7. sharecropper	G. stone to sharpen knives or tools
8. punctuated	H. low cry
9. sustained	I. emphasized; interrupted
10. whimper	J. experienced; maintained
11. whetstone	K. farmer who gives share of crop as rent
12. curiosity	L. great accuracy
13. regain	M. something handed down through generations
14. constrain	N. harshly firm
15. plaintive	O. hold in arms to show love
16. flounder	P. tree with orange-red, plum-like fruit
17. smokehouse	Q. animal chased in a hunt

Headliners

Use the vocabulary words from the first part of this activity to create three headlines. Use at least one vocabulary word (or a form of the word) per headline. Try to use more!

Example: **Victim Regains Stolen Property**

1.

2.

3.

Comprehension and Discussion Questions
Chapter One

Answer the following questions in complete sentence form. Give examples from the story to support your response.

1. Why doesn't the author give names to the human characters in the book?

_____

_____

_____

_____

2. The only name used is Sounder. Why is Sounder a good name for the family's dog? Present a short "word picture" of Sounder. Tell how he helps the family.

_____

_____

_____

_____

3. Why do the morning cooking smells remind the boy of Christmas?

_____

_____

_____

_____

4. Why does the boy's mother hum? Do you think that she has any reason for concern at this point? Explain.

_____

_____

_____

_____

Comprehension and Discussion Questions
Chapter Two

Answer the following questions in complete sentence form. Give examples from the story to support your response.

1. Why doesn't Sounder warn the family about the arrival of the sheriff and his deputies?

_____

_____

_____

_____

2. How do the men treat the boy's father during the arrest? Support your answer by giving examples of their words and actions. How does the family react to the arrest?

_____

_____

_____

_____

3. Do you think the father's crime is equal to his punishment? State reasons for your opinion.

_____

_____

_____

_____

4. How does Sounder try to help his master? What happens to him as a result?

_____

_____

_____

_____

Vocabulary
Chapters Three and Four

Use your dictionary to define the following words.

1. addled

2. caution

3. chute

4. corridor

5. crockery

6. foothills

7. gnaw

8. grieve

9. haunches

10. hesitated

11. rivulets

12. slacken

13. spiral

14. threadbare

Vocabulary
Chapters Seven and Eight

Use the words in the box to complete the sentences below. You may need to use your dictionary.

animosity	glee	mellow	cistern
gyration	persimmon	compulsion	hobbled
rivulet	conjure	jeer	sultry
	gaunt	malicious	

1. The _____ July weather was to be expected.

2. The _____ of the kite soon brought it crashing down.

3. Sandra was a _____ old woman; she was gentle and dignified.

4. The wounded horse _____ back to the stable.

5. The patient looked weak and _____ following the illness.

6. The _____ remained between the two enemies long after the argument had ended.

7. Mama's _____ jam won the blue ribbon at the county fair.

8. The boy went to the _____ to get water for his mother.

9. The comments made by the jealous crowd were _____.

10. When the child saw the stack of gifts, his face filled with _____.

11. When the batter struck out, the taunting fans began to _____.

12. The rainfall was so heavy that a new _____ was formed where no stream had existed.

13. Ed felt a _____ to complete all of his chores in one afternoon.

14. The secret chant was meant to _____ the spirits to the ceremony.

Comprehension and Discussion Questions
Chapter Seven

Answer the following questions in complete sentence form. Give examples from the story to support your response.

1. Why does the boy assume that his father is not among the prisoners who are whitewashing the rocks?

_____

_____

_____

_____

2. What does the boy find dumped in a barrel among the trash? Why does he carry it with him even though it makes his hand hurt more?

_____

_____

_____

_____

3. Do you think the boy is still impressed with the idea of schooling and with schools in general?

_____

_____

_____

_____

4. Which aspects of the teacher's home most impress the boy? Why?

_____

_____

_____

_____

Comprehension and Discussion Questions
Chapter Eight

Answer the following questions in complete sentence form. Give examples from the story to support your response.

1. Why does the mother warn her son to be careful about picking through the trash?

_____

_____

_____

_____

2. How does the author tell the readers that six years have elapsed since the father was arrested?

_____

_____

_____

_____

3. Animal behavior is used by the author to foreshadow an event. What is the event? Describe the animal behaviors used to foreshadow it.

_____

_____

_____

_____

4. Why is the boy's mother seemingly unconcerned that he will live with someone she does not know?

_____

_____

_____

_____

Spotlight Literary Skill
Mood

Mood is the feeling or effect that is created by the author's words. Settings, actions, characterizations and descriptions can all be written to convey certain moods. Read the following story selections and think about how the passages make you feel.

On the line below each selection, describe the mood that the author has created:

1. "Christmas bells were ringing in the town. . . . The people he saw were laughing and talking. . . . He looked at the store windows out of the corner of his eye. They were silvery and gold and green and red and sparkling."

_____

2. "The man with the red face squeezed the cake in his hands and broke it into four pieces. . . . Part of the cake fell to the floor; it was only a box of crumbs now."

_____

3. "The boy wanted to run after her. He watched as she became smaller and smaller, until the meal sack over her shoulder was just a white speck. . . . When the white speck had faded into the earth, the boy looked up at the sky."

_____

4. "The boy listened to the wind passing through the tops of the tall pines; he thought they moved like giant brooms sweeping the sky. The moonlight raced down the broken spaces of swaying trees and sent bright shafts of light along the ground and over him."

_____

5. "They buried the boy's father in the unfenced lot behind the meetin' house. The preacher stood amid the sumac and running briars before the mound of fresh red earth and read:

The Lord is my shepherd; I shall not want, He maketh me to lie down in green pastures."

_____

Spotlight Literary Skill
Fact and Opinion

A fact is a statement that can be proven. An opinion may be defined as a personal belief.

Examples:
Fact: Ice cream is made from cream and sugar.
Opinion: Chocolate ice cream is the most delicious.

Read each statement below. Decide if it is a fact or an opinion and place an "F" or an "O" in the space provided.

_____ 1. " 'It's a troublesome trip,' she said."

_____ 2. " 'For being hurt, they gave me time off my sentence.' "

_____ 3. " 'Sounder won't go mad,' the boy said."

_____ 4. " 'In all the books...there's no story as good as Joseph's story,' he would say."

_____ 5. "The loose boards did not rattle as the chair moved on them."

_____ 6. " 'Lots of old folks is conjured or addled.' "

_____ 7. " 'That's a school too,' he said to himself."

_____ 8. "The months and seasons of searching stretched into years."

_____ 9. "He thought the giant pines were like giant brooms sweeping the sky."

_____ 10. " 'You're a hard worker for your age.' "

_____ 11. "This is a wonderful book," said the teacher.

_____ 12. "He was bringing him a cake for Christmas."

_____ 13. "Church bells were ringing in the town."

_____ 14. "A mad dog is a fearful sight."

_____ 15. " 'This would have been a good hunting night,' he thought."

Spotlight Literary Skill
Plot: Sequencing

A **plot** is a sequence of events that tells a story. You have just read *Sounder*. Put the following events in the correct plot order (the order in which they occurred).

_____ The deputy shoots Sounder.

_____ The boy's mother returns the stolen goods.

_____ The teacher invites the boy to his cabin.

_____ Sounder crawls under the cabin and dies.

_____ The boy's injured father returns home to his family.

_____ The sheriff and deputy handcuff the boy's father and take him away in the wagon.

_____ The boy is surprised by the smell of sausage and hambone in the cabin.

_____ ''Tell her not to send you no more,'' said the boy's father at the end of his son's visit.

_____ Crippled and worn, Sounder finds his way back to the cabin.

_____ The boy finds an old book in the trash and tries to read it.

Rewrite the sentences in the proper sequence.

Spotlight Literary Skill
Cause and Effect

Sometimes a certain event or action brings about another event or action. This is what is meant by **cause and effect.** Read the following statement: The family had no food so the father stole a ham. The first part of the statement, ''The family had no food,'' is the cause. The second part, ''so the father stole a ham,'' is the effect. In other words, it is the lack of food that causes him to steal the ham.

Match the causes in the column on the left with the effects in the column on the right. Place the correct letter on each line.

CAUSES	EFFECTS
_____ 1. His little brother gets upset without him in the bed.	A. The boy does not attend school.
_____ 2. She respects his strength, courage and loyalty.	B. Sounder stays away for months.
_____ 3. It is far away and he is not encouraged.	C. Father and the family do not write to each other.
_____ 4. The camp moves all over the state; there is no communication.	D. The mother sometimes cares for Sounder herself.
_____ 5. Father leaves without Sounder one night.	E. The boy goes to bed before he is really tired.
_____ 6. No members of the family can read or write.	F. The boy, mother and dog think it is strange.
_____ 7. He has to recover from his terrible wounds.	G. The children think that he is a new student.
_____ 8. People throw newspapers and magazines into the trash.	H. The boy has materials with which to practice his reading.
_____ 9. He is in the schoolyard with a book.	I. Mother picks walnuts from the shells.
_____ 10. She knows she can sell them for food or cash.	J. The boy cannot find his father.

A Photo Album

Decide which four characters in the story are the most memorable. You certainly may include Sounder. Draw a "photograph" of each of those characters in one of the frames. Above the picture write the name of the character. On the lines below the picture, describe the character in words.

Man's Best Friend

Dogs have been affectionately referred to as "man's best friend." Dogs have been used as sentries, police dogs, messengers and lifeguards. They have also been trained to assist the blind and physically handicapped.

How did Sounder win the title "Man's Best Friend"? Write a newspaper article reporting Sounder's efforts to save his master. Although he was not successful, do you still consider him a hero? Why or why not? Explain your answer.

THE DAILY JOURNAL

_____
date

_____
headline

_____

_____

_____

_____

_____

_____

_____

_____

_____

Post-Reading Activity
What Happened Next?

Create a sequel to *Sounder.* What happens to the boy and his family? Do they continue to live as sharecroppers or does the boy's education change the family's way of life? What lasting memories of the father do they carry with them? What lasting memories of Sounder do they carry with them? Write a rough draft of your story in the space below. Give your story an imaginative title! Re-write your story on another sheet of paper and illustrate it.

Cooperative Learning Activities
Understanding Human Rights

1. The human rights of American citizens are written in the Constitution. They include the right of all citizens to enjoy life and liberty as Americans. Along with the other members of your Cooperative Learning Group, research the provisions of the U.S. Constitution and make a list of the variety of human rights that you find. Be sure to include the Bill of Rights and other amendments in your investigation.

   Select one constitutional human right from your list. Use it as the basis for a short skit. Present the skit to your classmates.

2. Some human rights are not specifically written into the Constitution. We all value the right to be treated fairly, with dignity and respect, regardless of race, religion or social status. With the members of your Cooperative Learning Group, discuss the ways in which the characters in *Sounder* suffered from the lack of these human rights. If this story were set in the present time, would the characters be treated differently? Why or why not?

Letter to the Editor

Letters to the editor of a newspaper are usually persuasive and opinionated. As a concerned citizen, you learn of the circumstances surrounding the boy's father's imprisonment. You write a letter to the editor. Your letter should include the facts surrounding his crime, arrest and imprisonment.

Dear Editor:

With your Cooperative Learning Group, brainstorm other political action or persuasive public attention strategies that could be taken to remedy the unfairness of the situation. List your ideas here.

Glossary of Literary Terms

Alliteration: A repetition of initial, or beginning, sounds in two or more consecutive or neighboring words.

Analogy: A comparison based upon the resemblance in some particular ways between things that are otherwise unlike.

Anecdote: A short account of an interesting, amusing or biographical occurrence.

Anticlimax: An event that concludes a series of events. It is less important than what has already occurred.

Archaic language: Language that was once common in a particular historic period but which is no longer commonly used.

Cause and effect: The relationship in which one condition brings about another condition as a direct result. The result, or consequence, is called the effect.

Character development: The ways in which the author shows how a character changes as the story proceeds.

Characterization: The method used by the author to give readers information about a character; a description or representation of a person's qualities or peculiarities.

Classify: To arrange according to a category or trait.

Climax: The moment when the action in a story reaches its greatest conflict.

Compare and contrast: To examine the likenesses and differences of two people, ideas or things. (Contrast always emphasizes differences. Compare may focus on likenesses alone or on likenesses and differences.)

Conflict: The main source of drama and tension in a literary work; the discord between persons or forces that brings about dramatic action.

Connotation: Something suggested or implied, not actually stated.

Description: An account that gives the reader a mental image or picture of something.

Dialect: A form of language used in a certain geographic region; it is distinguished from the standard form of the language by pronunciation, grammar and/or vocabulary.

Dialogue (dialog): The parts of a literary work that represent conversation.

Fact: A piece of information that can be proven or verified.

Figurative language: Description of one thing in terms usually used for something else. Simile and metaphor are examples of figurative language.

Flashback: The insertion of an earlier event into the normal chronological sequence of a narrative.

Foreshadowing: The use of clues to give readers a hint of events that will occur later on.

Historical fiction: Fiction represented in a setting true to the history of the time in which the story takes place.

Imagery: Language that appeals to the senses; the use of figures of speech or vivid descriptions to produce mental images.

Irony: The use of words to express the opposite of their literal meaning.

Legend: A story handed down from earlier times; its truth is popularly accepted but cannot be verified.

Limerick: A humorous five-lined poem with a specific form: aabba. Lines 1, 2 and 5 are longer than lines 3 and 4.

Metaphor: A figure of speech that compares two unlike things without the use of like or as.

Mood: The feeling that the author creates for the reader.

Motivation: The reasons for the behavior of a character.

Narrative: The type of writing that tells a story.

Narrator: The character who tells the story.

Opinion: A personal point of view or belief.

Parody: Writing that ridicules or imitates something more serious.

Personification: A figure of speech in which an inanimate object or an abstract idea is given human characteristics.

Play: A literary work that is written in dialogue form and that is usually performed before an audience.

Plot: The arrangement or sequence of events in a story.

Point of view: The perspective from which a story is told.

Protagonist: The main character.

Pun: A play on words that are similar in sound but different in meaning.

Realistic fiction: True-to-life fiction; the people, places and happenings are similar to those in real life.

Resolution: The part of the plot from the climax to the ending where the main dramatic conflict is worked out.

Satire: A literary work that pokes fun at individual or societal weaknesses.

Sequencing: The placement of story elements in the order of their occurrence.

Setting: The time and place in which the story occurs.

Simile: A figure of speech that uses *like* or *as* to compare two unlike things.

Stereotype: A character whose personality traits represent a group rather than an individual.

Suspense: Quality that causes readers to wonder what will happen next.

Symbolism: The use of a thing, character, object or idea to represent something else.

Synonyms: Words that are very similar in meaning.

Tall tale: An exaggerated story detailing unbelievable events.

Theme: The main idea of a literary work; the message the author wants to communicate, sometimes expressed as a generalization about life.

Tone: The quality or feeling conveyed by the work; the author's style or manner of expression.

ANSWERS

Chapters One and Two: Vocabulary

1. Q	6. L	11. G	16. B
2. P	7. K	12. F	17. A
3. O	8. I	13. E	
4. N	9. J	14. D	
5. M	10. H	15. C	

Chapter One: Comprehension and Discussion Questions (Answers may vary.)

1. The lack of names emphasizes the universal problem that blacks faced in the South at that time.

2. Sounder was probably named for his unusual bark. He is a mixture of Georgia redbone hound and bulldog. He has square jaws and head, a muscular neck and a broad chest.
He helps the family by bringing in food.

3. The last time that the boy recalls the smell of pork sausages was at Christmas. It is not a usual meal at their home.

4. She always hums when she is worried.
She may worry about where the father got the ham. Also she may wonder where he went without his dog or lantern.

Chapter Two: Comprehension and Discussion Questions (Answers may vary.)

1. Sounder had grown restless and had wandered away to hunt alone; therefore, he isn't at home when the men arrive to arrest his master.

2. They treat the father in a cruel way. His clothes are ripped; they strike him in the face; and they speak to him in an abusive manner. For example, one says, "Stick out your hands, boy."
The rest of the family seem helpless and restrained.

3. Answers will vary.

4. Sounder barks angrily and races after the wagon. The deputy shoots and wounds Sounder.

Chapter Three: Comprehension and Discussion Questions (Answers may vary.)

1. She knows that the food has been stolen and plans to return it.

2. The boy's cabin does not have curtains on the windows, so to him it is a special treat to see and feel them. They remind him of his mother's description of sea foam.

3. He waits until the wood in the stove burns down before he leaves the cabin. He keeps within hollering distance and warns the children not to open the stove door while the fire is strong.

4. After he fails to locate Sounder, he cries because of the loneliness of the moment. The terrible events of the day suddenly are more than he can bear.

Chapter Four: Comprehension and Discussion Questions (Answers may vary.)

1. She is preparing the boy for the possible loss of Sounder. She feels that people are fated to have good or bad lives.

2. This is his first trip to town alone and he is afraid that strangers will notice him and stop him. He is also anxious about meeting with his father and he hopes that he will not grieve him.

3. The man with the red face squeezes the cake and destroys it. He also makes the boy wait out in the cold and speaks to him in an unkind manner.
The boy wishes the man a violent death, like that of a bull in a cattle chute.

4. He doesn't want him to come because it upsets both him and his son.

Chapters Five and Six: Vocabulary

Part 1

1. a	3. a	5. b	7. a
2. a	4. c	6. c	8. b

Part 2

1. Different: b	3. Same	5. Different: c	7. Different: b
2. Same	4. Different: a	6. Different: a	8. Different: a

Chapter Five: Comprehension and Discussion Questions (Answers may vary.)

1. In their innocence, they may have asked questions which would have been painful for their mother to hear.

2. No one in the family can read or write. The idea of dictating letters to the traveling preacher does occur to them, but it is thought to be too complicated because they have no regular mail delivery.

3. She probably feels sorry for this creature in its suffering. Also, it was Sounder's attempt to protect her husband that caused him to be wounded.

4. Answers will vary.

Chapter Six: Comprehension and Discussion Questions (Answers may vary.)

1. He reminds her that many Bible stories are about individuals who went on perilous journeys and that some were even children like him.

2. The familiarity of the stories is comforting in itself. The stories all have happy endings, and the people in them are not afraid of anything.

3. The sounds of the wind in the trees remind him of the Bible story of King David in a similar situation. He imagines that David is there with him.

4. He finds newspapers and magazines that have been thrown away. He uses them to practice his reading. He enjoys the challenge and it is a way of passing time while waiting at the gates and fences, hoping for a glimpse of his father.

Chapters Seven and Eight: Vocabulary:

1. sultry	5. gaunt	9. malicious	13. compulsion
2. gyrations	6. animosity	10. glee	14. conjure
3. mellow	7. persimmon	11. jeer	
4. hobbled	8. cistern	12. rivulet	

Chapter Seven: Comprehension and Discussion Questions (Answers may vary.)

1. He believes that his father would have come to his defense. "'He ain't there,' the boy murmured to himself. If he was, the boy knew, by now he would be holding the scarecrow of a man in the air...."

2. He finds a book. Even though he does not understand the words, he cherishes it because "all his life he had wanted a book."

3. Yes, he is still in awe of schools and of attending school. He crosses the street so that he can observe the school as he walks. When he recognizes a black school, he stops and studies what is happening. Later the author writes, "The boy wanted to follow the man into the schoolhouse and see what it was like inside."

4. He is impressed that the cabin has a fenced-in grassy area. The ownership of so many books, two lamps and two stoves—one to cook on and one to warm by—makes an impression on the boy.

Chapter Eight: Comprehension and Discussion Questions (Answers may vary.)

1. She thinks he may be accused of stealing whatever he happens to find in the trash. She knows it would cause a great deal of trouble for all of them.

2. He writes, "Six crops of persimmons and wild grapes had ripened." These crops mature only once per year.

3. The event is the return of the father. The animal behaviors include the following: Sounder hobbles back and forth down to the road several times; a catbird fusses; a mockingbird calls from the top of a tall locust tree; Sounder comes from under the porch and begins to whine; and eventually, Sounder runs to the figure and begins to bark.

4. She believes that this invitation is an opportunity ordained by the Lord. She knows it is the only chance her son has for a better life.

Spotlight Skill: Mood

1. happy   2. angry   3. frightened, worried   4. lonely   5. sad

Spotlight Skill: Fact and Opinion

1. O	4. O	7. F	10. O	13. F
2. F	5. F	8. F	11. O	14. O
3. O	6. O	9. O	12. F	15. O

Spotlight Skill: Plot

The sentences should be written in the following order: 3 - 4 - 8 - 10 - 9 - 2 - 1 - 5 - 6 - 7

Spotlight Skill: Cause and Effect

1. E   2. D   3. A   4. J   5. F   6. C   7. B   8. H   9. G   10. I